PANORAMA

A HISTORY *OF*

FASHION

FROM LOINCLOTHS *TO* LYCRA

Author:
Jacqueline Morley is a graduate of Oxford University. She has taught English and History, and now works as a freelance translator and writer with a special interest in the history of everyday life. She has written historical fiction and nonfiction for children. She assisted in the installation of the costume display at Warwick County Museum and advised on the Fashion Gallery at Brighton Museum in Brighton.

Series designer:
David Salariya was born in Dundee, Scotland, where he studied illustration and printmaking, concentrating on book design in his post-graduate year. He later completed a further post-graduate course in art education at Sussex University. He has illustrated a wide range of books on botanical, historical and mythical subjects. He has designed and created many new series of children's books for publishers in the UK and overseas, including the award-winning **Inside Story** series. He lives in Brighton with his wife, the illustrator Shirley Willis.

Consultant:
Rosemary Harden is keeper of collections at the Museum of Costume and Fashion Research Centre, Bath, where she looks after a collection of well over 20,000 items of fashionable dress from the late 17th century to the present day.

Series designer: David Salariya
Editor: Penny Clarke
Consultant: Rosemary Harden
Artists: David Antram
Virginia Gray
Gerald Wood

Illustrations by:
David Antram 18-19, 20-21, 22-23, 24-25, 26-27, 28-29; **Virginia Gray** 30-31, 32-33, 34-35, 36-37, 38-39, 40-41, 42-43; **Gerald Wood** 8-9, 10-11, 12-13, 14-15, 16-17.

First published in 1995, and reprinted in 1997, by Macdonald Young Books, an imprint of Wayland Publishers Ltd
61, Western Road, Hove
East Sussex, BN3 1JD

ISBN 0-7500-1588-8

© The Salariya Book Co Ltd MCMXCV

Printed in Portugal by Edições ASA

A CIP catalogue record for this book is available from the British Library

PANORAMA

A HISTORY OF

FASHION

FROM LOINCLOTHS TO LYCRA

Written by
JACQUELINE MORLEY

Created & Designed by
DAVID SALARIYA

MACDONALD YOUNG BOOKS

CONTENTS

INTRODUCTION

Suppose we all dressed alike? Would it make any difference to our lives? They would certainly be duller – less to look at, to talk about and to plan for, because clothes are important to us. Even people who say they never think about clothes would not go out in anything that made them feel silly, so, whether they realize it or not, they do think about what they wear.

Dressing alike would alter the way we buy clothes. We would use them till they wore out and then get replacements. The reason that we do not

do this, if we can afford not to, is that something called 'fashion' makes us dissatisfied with the clothes we have and so we buy new ones.

Because we can choose what we wear, and people see what we have chosen, our clothes say a lot about us. Way-out styles, or stuffy ones, reveal our characters, office and work clothes show what

we do, designer labels prove we have money, smart clothes show we have an eye for style.

But who decides what is fashionable? And who decided in the past? This book looks at clothes, from long ago until today, to see how people dressed, how much choice they had, and when the idea of 'keeping up with fashion' became important.

2500 BC

2500 BC

1500 BC

cone of
scented wax

900 BC

wig

putting on
the shift

tying
it up

ANCIENT TIMES

Minoan gold pin in daisy form, c2000 BC. The goldsmiths of the ancient world were highly skilled.

The idea that our way of dressing should be liable to frequent changes is quite a modern one. In the distant past, when people had to spin thread and weave cloth by hand before they could make a garment, they wanted their clothes to last as long as possible. Great rulers, of course, had their clothes made for them. The pharaohs of ancient Egypt and the emperors of Babylonia and Assyria had many luxurious garments and wore magnificent jewellery. Their subjects expected them to do so. The grandeur of their monarchs' clothes expressed the glory of their nation. Ordinary people wore clothes appropriate to the work they did, for example as priest, labourer or soldier. They did not expect the look of these to change. They assumed that everything in the world would remain as it was, since the gods had made it so. This way of looking at things lasted for thousands of years.

These early clothes were made of draped cloth, in the form of loincloths or longer wrapped skirts, and shawls, a tradition continued by the ancient Greeks and Romans. The early Romans admired simplicity in dress, but by the time of the Empire in the 2nd century BC increasing wealth had given people an appetite for gold jewellery and luxurious patterned togas of eastern silk.

Egyptians wore white linen shifts or loincloths for three thousand years. Styles changed so slowly that no one would have noticed in a lifetime.

Egyptian woman c1500 BC, in a wide shift of fine linen draped and tied over a narrow linen sheath. The cone of scented wax is to refresh her.

jewelled collar

Egyptians loved jewellery, especially necklaces. The rich wore gold and precious stones, the poor used beads.

ring

ear stud

necklace with
sacred scarab
beetle

Sandals were the only footwear. Even rich people frequently went barefoot.

550 BC   450 BC   350 BC   100 BC

▲ GREEK WOMAN, c400 BC, wearing a long wide tunic of fine linen, softly draped, and an all-enveloping rectangular cloak, also worn by men.

▲ ROMAN WOMEN'S hairstyles: from top left, for an older woman or widow; a Grecian style; Egyptian influence; an elaborate style of imperial Rome, cAD 150.

ROMAN in a toga and short tunic, 1st century AD. Originally the toga had been worn over a loincloth only.

The typical Roman garment was the toga.

The purple band on this toga shows that its wearer is a priest or magistrate. Ordinary citizens wore plain white togas.

ONE END of the toga crossed the shoulders and hung down to the left foot in front. The rest was wrapped round the body in various ways.

▲ GRADUALLY the toga became so voluminous that it restricted activity. It became an upperclass garment. Working people wore tunics.

2500 BC Priest and queen from Sumeria, an ancient civilization in part of modern Iraq.

2500 BC Ancient Egyptian. The rigid pleats of his loincloth show that he is a person of importance.

1500 BC Minoan prince and attendant. The Minoans of Crete had a civilization almost as old as the Egyptians. Men wore tightly belted loincloths, and women bell-shaped skirts with tight waists.

900 BC Assyrian ruler and attendant. The king's tightly curled hair and beard is a sign of rank. Assyria, too, was an ancient civilization in part of modern Iraq.

550 BC Greek couple wearing tunics called chitons. Made from oblongs of fabric, chitons were fastened by brooches at the shoulders. The woman's is doubled over at the top to form a drape.

450 BC Greek huntsman with a short cloak and wide-brimmed hat.

350 BC A Scythian couple. The Scythian nomads of the steppes north of the Black Sea wore close-fitting garments and trousers, suited to their life on horseback. The Persians, also horsemen, had introduced the trouser element of this costume to the Middle East in the 6th century. The Greeks and Romans regarded trousers as barbaric garments, not suited to settled, civilized life.

100 BC Roman family. Roman women wore a long tunic, and, outdoors, a large draped cloak, covering the head.

Byzantium and The Dark Ages

6th-century silver sandal discovered in a tomb in Switzerland. It would be for ceremonial use only.

BYZANTINE EMPRESS of the 6th century in silk robes, woven with gold thread and set with precious stones. Until this time silk had been imported, as only China had silkworms, which it guarded jealously. In the 6th century some silkworms were smuggled out to Constantinople, which set up its own silk industry.

Imperial diadem of gold set with pearls and emeralds. Ropes of pearls, ending in huge pearl drops, hang from it.

The Roman

Empire was divided in the 4th century. Rome remained the capital of the western half; the eastern capital was a new city built by the Emperor Constantine (cAD 280-337) at Byzantium. It was called Constantinople after him. In the 5th century the western empire was overcome by northern barbarians, horribly dressed to Roman eyes in coarse tunics and trousers or braies. The Byzantine empire lasted another thousand years.

Constantinople was an immensely rich city. It controlled the great trade routes between east and west. Silks, spices and precious stones from Persia, India and China were sold in its teeming markets. These riches affected Byzantine dress. It became stiff and magnificent, combining classical Roman draping with splendid eastern silks, embroidered ornament and jewels. The costliest fabrics were reserved for the emperor and his family.

For much of this time, western Europe was too lawless and afflicted by wars for people to worry about the way they dressed. Travel became unsafe so trade declined, and since there was nothing exciting to buy, fashion stagnated and died. Men and women wore simple tunics and overtunics, with cloaks for out of doors. There were few changes in clothes until late in the 12th century, when conditions began to become more settled.

Band of woven decoration.

AD 900   AD 997   AD 1070   AD 1150   AD 1170

BYZANTINE EMPEROR of the 6th century in a gold-embroidered silk tunic and a long cloak with an inset square decoration, or tablion. Only the imperial family and the highest court officials could wear this.

Crown decorated with pearl pendants.

Silk cloak lined with contrasting silk.

THE EMPEROR wears shaped leg coverings and soft shoes with ankle decoration.

MEROVINGIAN brooch, 6th or 7th century, made of bronze strips applied to a metal base to form compartments which were filled with enamel. Jewellery made by this technique, called 'cloisonné', was highly prized. Below, cloisonné buckle of the same date.

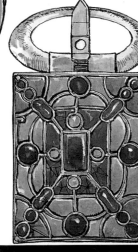

AD 375 Roman couple. The toga is now much narrower. The woman wears a wide-sleeved tunic called a dalmatic, first worn in Rome in the 2nd century AD. She has a large head veil, and her cloak is draped like a stole.

AD 400 Byzantine official. He wears military clothes and his cloak is fastened on one shoulder to leave the sword arm free. Cloaks had replaced togas.

AD 560 A Byzantine noblewoman and a man in travelling clothes. Her tight-sleeved undertunic is almost hidden by a silk overtunic and an elaborately draped and belted cloak. The man's patterned trousers are Persian in style.

AD 800 Anglo-Saxons. The men wear wide-sleeved overtunics with decorated borders. Women wore coverchiefs over their hair in public.

AD 900 Viking woman in an open-sided overdress with shoulder straps. The Viking merchant's fur hat and baggy trousers are influenced by Slav clothes of eastern Europe.

AD 997 Otto II, Emperor of the Franks, in long ceremonial robes.

AD 1070 Norman woman.

AD 1150 Norman nobleman and noblewoman. In the 12th century lacing was used to shape tunics much more closely to the body, and sleeves widened out enormously at the wrist.

AD 1170 Three-quarter-length fur overtunic, front-slit for riding.

1230 1240 1250 1280 1317

wimple

THE MIDDLE AGES

Venetian gold belt end. Men and women wore belts from which they hung their purses.

By the 13th century Europe was reasonably peaceful. The Church and the rulers were strong enough to see that laws were obeyed. Towns, cathedrals and universities had grown up, and merchants travelled again, within Europe and beyond. Imported luxuries changed hands at huge fairs held in northern France, where traders from the south bringing Spanish leather, Italian and oriental silks and rare dyestuffs met those from the north selling fine woollen cloth and furs. These goods then found their way to markets throughout Europe.

Ideas for using these materials spread in the same way, so that new styles appeared all over Europe at about the same time. In the 13th century men wore long tunics with loose sleeves and sleeveless overtunics. In the 14th century men's garments changed. The tunic became close-fitting, with knee-length skirts (the forerunner of the doublet). The overtunic changed into the cote-hardie, another long garment with sleeves. Women also wore a version of the cote-hardie over the long, close-fitting dress known as the kirtle. The tailoring skills that these styles needed probably came from the east. Eastern textiles and craftsmanship had been admired in the west since the time of the first Crusade in the 11th century.

NOBLEWOMAN, c1330, in a fur-lined overtunic called a pelisson. It has a large attached hood, falling like a cape, which could be buttoned up to the throat, though the tiny buttons look more ornamental than useful.

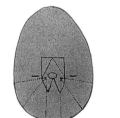

cut and shape of pelisson

THE PELISSON had the head hole towards one end, so that most of the fabric hung behind in a train.

FIGURE FROM a funeral monument, showing how a wimple filled the neckline and was held taut across the throat by being pinned to the hair.

1330   1350   1365   1380   1395

SINCE THE Dark Ages men had worn sock-like leg-wear, called hose, pulled up to meet their braies. Braies had got shorter and hose longer over the years.

doublet

eyelets

braies

How a hose-leg was shaped from a piece of cloth. Thigh-length hose had been held up by garters and probably sagged a lot. The new short fashions tended to reveal the braies, which were now regarded as underwear. The solution was to make the hose long enough to cover them. Each leg now came up over the braies and was held by laces passed through eyelet holes in the bottom of the doublet.

laces

hose

FASHIONABLE MEN put their heads into the face holes of their hoods and wound the long liripipe round their heads. Hats copied the style.

Hose might have soles attached to serve as shoes. In the 14th century hose often had long toes, padded to keep their shape, in keeping with the fashion for shoes with very long points.

WOMEN wore a barbette (a linen band) under the chin, often with a decorated hairnet (later called a crespine).

shoe with cut-out decoration

1230 Under his fur-trimmed cap the man has a coif (a linen bonnet fastened under the chin). The woman wears a crispine and barbette.

1240 The loose hair of this young woman shows she is unmarried.

1250 A new type of overgarment. The sleeves hang empty, while the arms pass through slits at the top.

1280 Woman in a close-fitting unbelted gown, flaring to a wide hem. A wimple covers her throat.

1317 Open-sided garments. The man's is open from shoulder to hem, the woman's is cut away at the sides. The man's tunic is dagged (cut out) along its edges, and so is the cape of his hood. He holds the liripipe, the long end, of his hood.

1330 Noblewoman in a fitted gown with laced sides.

1350 Noble couple, the man wearing the short fitted overgarment which had replaced the tunic. The woman's overgown is so cut away that nothing but a strip remains in front.

1365 Italian couple. The man's hemline is fashionably short. The woman wears a figure-hugging overgown.

1380 Man in a dagged houppelande, an overgarment which had appeared in the last twenty years. Worn by both sexes, they made cloaks unnecessary.

1395 North Italian woman in a houppelande with bold sleeves.

1416

1430

1448

1450

THE END OF THE MIDDLE AGES

Brooch of gold, enamel and pearls, c1450. Women set brooches in their hair. Men wore them in their hats.

Merchants and townspeople had been getting richer since the 14th century, and some could now lend money to princes. Lavish spending on silks, furs and jewellery was a sign of success and competition between the newly rich boosted fashion. Fashions in the 15th century took previous trends to extremes. Women's head-dresses curved up into horns, becoming wider and then exaggeratedly high. Men's garments became even shorter, with padded shoulders and sleeves. Shoe-points were kept off the ground by wooden pattens. Towards the end of the century young men wore doublets without any overgown, which was thought shocking. But complaints about fashion were nothing new. Long sleeves in the 12th century, low necks in the 13th, men's short skirts in the 14th, had all been denounced by the Church and sober-minded people. New fashions always cause disapproval somewhere.

Gold, jewels and costly fabrics were symbols of rank and power. When merchants and townspeople took to wearing them it marked an important change in society. Rulers tried to keep distinctions of rank by passing laws, called sumptuary laws, stating what each class of person could wear, but these were never obeyed for long.

AN ARTIST SKETCHED these young men around 1450. Each was dressed in the height of fashion, but a quick glance showed that the man on the left was Italian, in the centre German, and on the right, Burgundian.

THE HENNIN, a tall conical cap, had a floating veil, often held out over a wire frame.

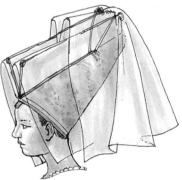

ITALIAN HAIRSTYLE, 1465, coiled with ribbons, and held with jewelled pins. Tall headgear was a northern fashion.

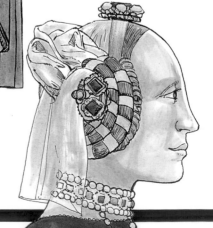

↑ THIS GOWN OF 1435 is the height of fashion, and so is the wearer's stance, with hips thrust forward and skirt held up over her stomach.

1460

1490

1495

fringed hair, bound with a fillet

hanging sleeve thrown over arm

Burgundian cropped hair and hat

doublet sleeve

doublet

overgown

dagged edging

hose of different colours

1416 Elegant Burgundian courtiers. The man wears a houppelande and the woman a low-necked gown and plumed fur hat.

1430 Italian couple. Both show the vogue for garments with ample folds, and a turban-like silhouette on the head. Women could achieve this by dressing their hair over a frame.

1448 Philip the Good, Duke of Burgundy, and his young son, wearing richly patterned velvet overgowns hanging in regular folds that must have been held by stitching. The courtier with them has a longer gown of the kind worn by older men, but his haircut and pointed footgear with pattens are modish.

1450 French noblewoman in the most outlandish of the century's elaborate head-dresses. Her ermine-trimmed gown is open, above a high, broad belt, to display the undergown.

1460 Burgundian fashions for the young and elegant. The man's overtunic is daringly short; his shoulders, chest and sleeves are padded, and he dangles an extra hat over his shoulder on the end of a liripipe. The woman has a new version of the horned head-dress, with a liripipe, copied from men's fashion.

1490 Flemish couple. The broad fur collar of his open-sided cape produces a wide-shouldered silhouette. His shoes are fashionably blunt-toed.

1495 Three Venetians. The man on the right wears a brief doublet with no overgarment.

1514   1535   1538   1546   1550   1555

THE 16TH CENTURY

Man's leather glove, c1530, with embroidered satin cuffs edged with gold metal thread lace.

In the 16th century clothes in Europe were made of sumptuous fabrics, such as patterned silk, velvets richly decorated with jewels, lace and lavish embroidery. The influence of the Renaissance, which had begun in Italy in the 15th century and celebrated the rebirth of learning and harmony, continued. This spirit extended beyond painting and architecture to fashionable dress.

In the first half of the century rich men from northern Europe wore cloaks with wide shoulders and flat hats, giving them a very square appearance. In the second half they followed the fashions of Spain (whose wealth from silver mines in the New World made it Europe's leading power) and wore trunk hose padded round their thighs like balloons and doublets with high necks. Doublet padding moved from shoulders to stomach, producing a peculiarly overhanging 'peascod' belly. Shirt-neck frills developed into the starched ruffs worn by both sexes.

Women achieved the fashionable triangular shape by wearing bodices or corsets stiffened with wood or metal. Skirts were supported by the Spanish farthingale, an underskirt held out by cane hoops. Towards 1600 a French version of the farthingale, shaped like a wheel, came into fashion in northern Europe.

French nobleman of the 1520s. The wide-shouldered doublet sleeves and the loose top gown with wide turn-back collar make a totally square shape.

flat cap with feather

shirt frill, which later became the ruff

jerkin

doublet sleeves

codpiece

upper hose

shirt pulled through

nether hose

broad-toed shoes with slashing

His doublet and upper hose are slashed. Slashing (cutting slits and pulling through the layer beneath) was used throughout the century. A jerkin with a wide V-neck is worn over the doublet. Each hose leg is now made of an upper and a nether (lower) half. A pouch called a codpiece fills the gap between the legs.

16

1560

1571

1581

1588

1595

ruff of fine cotton supported by a wire frame

lace ruff, open at the throat

open hanging sleeves

SMALL BOY, c1590, in ruff and hanging sleeves, like an adult. Boys wore skirts until they were about five.

ELIZABETH I of England in 1592. Her jewel-encrusted dress has the long-bodied outline with the wide skirt of contemporary fashion in its extreme form.

She wears a French farthingale, a large cane or metal hoop that stuck out horizontally at hip level. The pointed bodice front was held rigid by inserting a busk, a long strip of wood, metal or whalebone.

1514 Couple from Germany, where slashing was very fashionable.

1535 A wide neckline curves into the armpits. The rigid bodice is still short.

1538 Merchant in a long fur-lined gown. Long garments suggested dignity and ceremony. They were worn by officials, lawyers, doctors and churchmen, and elderly men.

1546 English nobleman wearing a doublet with a skirt and a stiff fur-lined gown with hanging sleeves.

1550 Gowns were now made in two parts – a stiffened bodice and a skirt. The skirt, open to show a decorative underskirt, is held rigid by a farthingale.

1555 Spaniard in richly patterned short gown worn like a cloak, and trunk hose (short wide upper hose stuffed with padding).

1560 Italian fashions were not as extreme as elsewhere in Europe.

1571 Spanish noblewoman in gold-embroidered velvet gown, with open sleeves tied at the wrist.

1581 French couple. An open ruff shows off the woman's throat.

1588 A fashionable young man wearing a padded 'peascod' doublet.

1595 Man in formal clothes, and boy in informal breeches and 'falling collar'. As often happens, these informal clothes became high fashion in a few years.

1618   1634   1640   1645   1646

THE 17TH CENTURY

Man's open ruff, 1618, and wire support. It replaced the round ruff of the 16th century.

As Spanish

political power waned, so their fashions, such as the farthingale, disappeared. Ruffs gradually changed from stiff cartwheels to supported collars and falling linen bands edged with fine lace. Above all, the powerful French court of Louis XIV set the fashions during the first half of the century.

For most of the 17th century women's clothes were restrained. Gowns of plain silks had wide necklines with a separate broad collar of lace. Towards 1700 the general effect became narrower and stiffer.

Long-skirted at first, men's doublets were short again by the 1640s, showing the shirt. Boots had 'bucket' tops filled with lace, and hair was worn in tumbling curls. Around 1660 there was a vogue for enormously wide 'petticoat' breeches like a skirt, with ribbons at waist and hem. Wigs gave yet longer curls, and huge lace flounces decked the wrists and knees. Such excesses justified the views of those people who rejected fashion on religious grounds, dressing plainly in black, a custom seen in Holland, and in England under the Puritans from 1649 to 1660.

Fashion loves extremes. After petticoat breeches, men wore a simple buttoned garment, the vest, worn with narrow breeches and a coat – the earliest form of the three-piece suit!

Dutch family, 1621. Their clothes are of dark, sumptuous, fabrics. The Dutch were a prosperous nation, newly independent of Spain.

falling collar

the apron shows this is a girl

THE ROUND RUFF was worn longer in Holland than elsewhere. The jutting stomacher is Dutch too. It may have been a fad, or a way of making fashion compatible with pregnancy.

Man's shoe, 1620. It was tied with ribbon and a big rosette.

1660   1663   1674   1678   1683   1693   1693

FASHION OF 1665.
The man wears petticoat
breeches and an open-
sleeved doublet, left
undone to show his
shirt. His hair is his
own. Wigs were still
a novelty.

*Women's hair
was simply
dressed, with
ringlets. A
single rope of
pearls was
popular.*

loops of ribbon
as trimming

LITTLE SILK parasols for
shading the face were a
novelty of the 1670s
which remained a fashion
favourite. Umbrellas for
rain were not used until
the next century.

*The woman's bodice (below)
and silk skirt are made
separately. Full three-
quarter sleeves were
usual. The low neck
was sometimes filled
with a separate
collar of fine
cotton or lace.*

CORSETS were shorter,
whalebone-stiffened, back-
laced, and with adjustable
shoulder straps. Whale-
bone slotted into two
pouches kept the neckline
rigid. A busk was inserted
in front. Sometimes the
bodice was boned and
acted as a corset.

1618 Loose-fitting breeches, open ruff,
and shoes with large rosettes as worn by
elegant young men.

1634 Family group. Men's hair is worn
longer. The doublet has become high-
waisted and the open ruff has drooped to
become a falling collar. Women's gowns
have higher waists and full soft skirts held
out by hip pads.

1640 Frenchman in bucket-topped
boots, narrower breeches decorated at the
hem and a high-waisted doublet.

1645 Frenchwoman with her skirt
drawn up to show the underskirt.

1646 Men's hair is even longer.
Breeches are decked with loops of ribbon.
Very short doublets show billows of shirt.

1660 Petticoat breeches. These were
mainly worn at court.

1663 The height of male display: the
doublet is smothered in buttons and
ribbons, and the lining of the breeches
ends in cascades of lace below the knees.

1674 For women a new outline:
narrower and stiffer. Ornamental aprons
are in fashion.

1678 Frenchman in a fitted coat.

1683 In winter a greatcoat went over
the coat.

1693 Woman's hunting costume
copying masculine fashion, including the
hair and hat.

1693 French couple in walking clothes.

1706   1720   1747   1749

THE 18TH CENTURY

Woman's embroidered shoe, 1715. (Right) Whaleboned corset, c1740.

At the beginning of the 18th century the well-dressed man wore a full-skirted coat, waistcoat (the 17th-century vest), narrow breeches, a wig (powdered white) and a three-cornered cocked hat. Coat and waistcoat were generally made of woven, patterned silk or richly embroidered. Fashions for men changed little until the 1760s when coats became narrower and cut away at the front. Then Englishmen started a fashion that was copied all over Europe, including France – they wore their comfortable country clothes in town! The coat with a turn-down collar known as a frock coat, a round hat (forerunner of the top hat) and riding boots became elegant wear.

Women's shapes went through amazing changes. Gowns, stiff and narrow-shouldered in 1700, became loose and billowy. The 'sack' dress, with a train from the shoulders, appeared in the 1720s and was popular for most of the century. Petticoats reinforced with hoops (like the farthingale but wider and flatter) or panniers that sat on the hips were used to create increasingly wide skirts, at their widest around 1750. Then they went out of fashion, except at court. Exaggerated fashions often end abruptly – when the smart world is all dressed in a certain way, it suddenly becomes ultra-smart to be different.

cocked hat

bag for tail of wig

coat of silk velvet

satin waistcoat

ENGLISHMAN OF 1747 in clothes typical of a gentleman's dress in the first half of the century.

silk stockings, pulled over breeches

buckled shoes

HIS EMBROIDERED COAT has deep cuffs and a full skirt with side pleats. His waistcoat is now rather shorter.

IN THE FIRST HALF of the century sumptuous fabrics were more important to men than fit. Coats were loose-fitting. Breeches were baggy in the seat, with let-down front flaps.

1759

1770

1771   1777

1781

1786

collapsible panniers

PANNIERS were made of cane or metal and were tied around the waist. Collapsible ones made going through doors easier.

THE WOMAN wears riding dress: a jacket with a turn-down collar like a man's and a plain skirt. Women borrowed men's styles for riding.

ENGLISH landowning family, c1767. The man is dressed informally in a plain woollen coat and waistcoat. The cut-away coat-skirt is convenient for riding. The woman's hat is like a man's country hat with added plumes.

FORMAL FRENCH suit of the 1790s. Though it is magnificently embroidered in silk, its shape is like the English country coat of 30 years earlier.

1706 Early in the century women's dresses were stiff tiers of flounces.

1720 A group of French aristocrats. The man's coat has stiffened skirts. The women wear sack dresses, open at the front and falling in loose pleats behind.

1747 Englishwoman in a plain gown worn over a hooped petticoat.

1749 Lifting the panniers.

1759 By now elegant Frenchwomen had decided that exaggerated panniers were old-fashioned for daytime wear. Lighter weight silks, profusely trimmed, gave a fullness that moved more naturally. Men's coats were less full-skirted.

1770 Formal French court dress. Panniers remained the correct wear at all European courts. The fantastic hairstyle is typical of the 1770s, a reaction to the neat close curls of earlier in the century.

1771 Formally dressed Englishman. His coat is more tightly fitted, and cut away at the sides.

1777 French walking costume. The skirt is caught up at the back, in a style known as a 'polonaise'.

1781 Englishman in the latest smart casual wear for town – a country coat, riding boots and a round-brimmed hat.

1786 French couple. The man's riding coat is a French version of the English style. The woman wears a chemise dress, a muslin shift like an undergarment, belted at the waist.

1790   1790   1794   1794   1796

REVOLUTION: 1789 TO 1815

Lafayette

French coat buttons, 1790, from a set showing leading figures of the Revolution.

Mirabeau

The vogue for simplicity, which in the 1780s had led grand ladies to wear plain white cotton gowns, was fashion's reflection of people's new interest in freedom, equality, and the simple natural life. The French Revolution (1789-99), which tried to put some of these ideas into practice, had a profound effect on dress. Styles associated with royalty – powdered hair, costly silks, formal panniers – became unpopular. Some extremists copied working men and wore loose trousers instead of tight breeches.

By 1794 the violent phase of the Revolution was over and Paris returned to fashionable living. Women wore slim high-waisted dresses of thinnest cotton, with low necks and tiny sleeves inspired by classical statues, because the Greek and Roman republics were associated with freedom. Women dampened filmy muslin dresses to make them cling like classical drapery.

Richer classical styles came into favour in 1804 when Napoleon Bonaparte became Emperor of France, because they reminded people of Imperial Rome. Fabrics became very luxurious and skirts began to widen at the hem.

Throughout this time well-fitting English clothes in plain cloth were the model for men everywhere.

In the 18th century England had been regarded on the Continent as the home of political freedom. This helped to give plain English styles their appeal abroad.

This mannered way of dressing, with hair in a tousled mop, a huge stand-up collar and a neckcloth that covered the chin, was adopted by some Frenchmen in the uncertain times just after the Revolution.

huge lapels

short waistcoat

skin-tight breeches

extra-long coat tails

The cut of this French coat is deliberately exaggerated. It does not have the understated look for which English tailoring was admired abroad.

THE HIGH-CROWNED hat is trimmed with a broad ribbon buckled in front. Its wide brim curves up at each side.

flat-heeled shoes

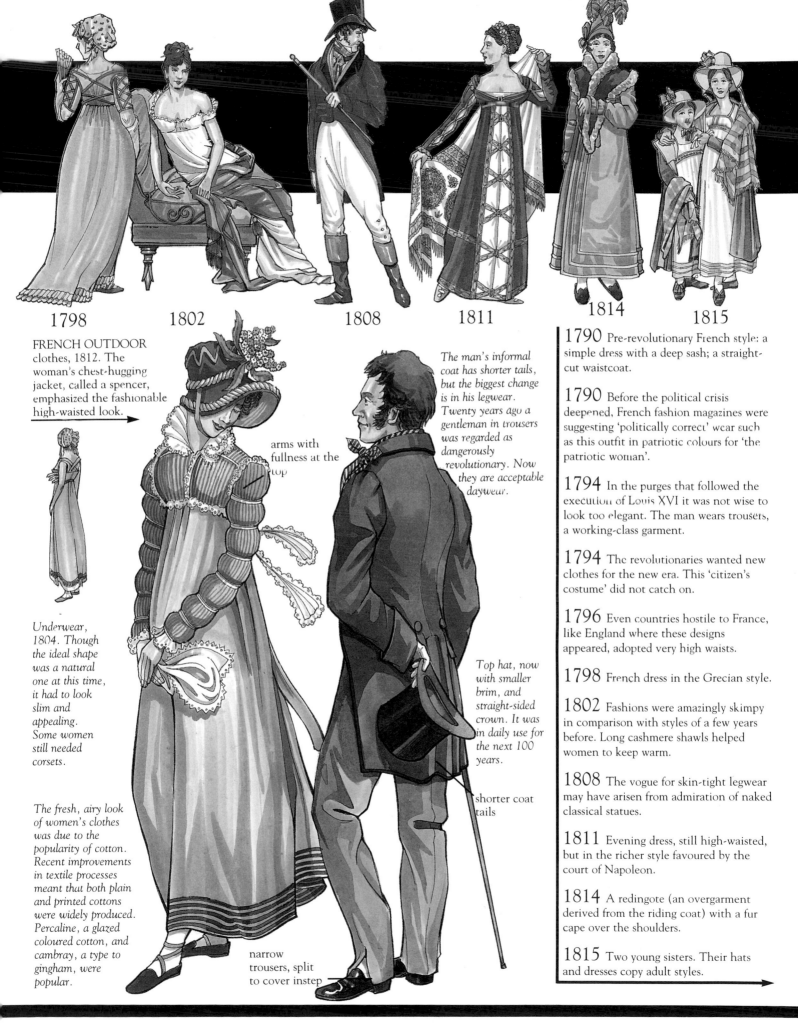

1798   1802   1808   1811   1814   1815

FRENCH OUTDOOR clothes, 1812. The woman's chest-hugging jacket, called a spencer, emphasized the fashionable high-waisted look.

Underwear, 1804. Though the ideal shape was a natural one at this time, it had to look slim and appealing. Some women still needed corsets.

The fresh, airy look of women's clothes was due to the popularity of cotton. Recent improvements in textile processes meant that both plain and printed cottons were widely produced. Percaline, a glazed coloured cotton, and cambray, a type to gingham, were popular.

arms with fullness at the top

The man's informal coat has shorter tails, but the biggest change is in his legwear. Twenty years ago a gentleman in trousers was regarded as dangerously revolutionary. Now they are acceptable daywear.

Top hat, now with smaller brim, and straight-sided crown. It was in daily use for the next 100 years.

shorter coat tails

narrow trousers, split to cover instep

1790 Pre-revolutionary French style: a simple dress with a deep sash; a straight-cut waistcoat.

1790 Before the political crisis deepened, French fashion magazines were suggesting 'politically correct' wear such as this outfit in patriotic colours for 'the patriotic woman'.

1794 In the purges that followed the execution of Louis XVI it was not wise to look too elegant. The man wears trousers, a working-class garment.

1794 The revolutionaries wanted new clothes for the new era. This 'citizen's costume' did not catch on.

1796 Even countries hostile to France, like England where these designs appeared, adopted very high waists.

1798 French dress in the Grecian style.

1802 Fashions were amazingly skimpy in comparison with styles of a few years before. Long cashmere shawls helped women to keep warm.

1808 The vogue for skin-tight legwear may have arisen from admiration of naked classical statues.

1811 Evening dress, still high-waisted, but in the richer style favoured by the court of Napoleon.

1814 A redingote (an overgarment derived from the riding coat) with a fur cape over the shoulders.

1815 Two young sisters. Their hats and dresses copy adult styles.

1817   1823   1828   1829   1829   1829   1830

THE EARLY 19TH CENTURY

An elegantly knotted cravat was essential. The wearer was judged by how well he tied it.

Before the 19th century fashion was decided by rulers and their courtiers, and rich people always copied the court. After Napoleon's defeat and exile in 1815, no European court was sufficiently dazzling to dictate a style. Instead, a powerful new middle class which had become rich through trade and manufacturing was eager to spend money on clothes and to impress others. More fashion journals appeared, describing the latest trends and where to buy fabrics and accessories.

Women's dress lost its slender simplicity after 1815. Skirts widened, and heavier printed cottons and silks replaced lightweight muslins. Waistlines dropped and by 1827 were back in the normal place. The waist had to be small. Both men and women wore corsets to nip it in. Men's full-skirted coats with padded sleeves were designed to emphasize the small waist.

In the late 1820s women's styles were jaunty, with bold trimmings, flirtatious hairstyles and deep-crowned bonnets with wide, face-framing brims, to which, in the 1830s, were added preposterously large sleeves. Following these flamboyant styles, fashion became sedate. By the 1840s dresses were plainer and faces hidden by little bonnets. Only skirts were eye-catching. They were becoming ever wider.

top hat, widening towards the crown

tall fur collar

Evening wear, 1828: an opera cloak, tail coat and pantaloons (skin-tight trousers).

Cartoon making fun of men's obsession with their figures, 1819. Few went to this extreme, but a trim figure and skilful tailoring were important now that men's fashions were so close-fitting.

The cloak's air of mystery and historical fancy dress reflects the 'romantic' mood of 1815 to 1835, when people loved to read about wild heroes and enjoyed the historical novels of Sir Walter Scott and Victor Hugo. Women's fashions were also affected, with turbans and collars suggesting ruffs.

silk socks and soft leather pumps

1833   1834   1836   1837   1840   1845   1847

artificial hairpiece

hair dressed with ribbon and sprays of artificial leaves

padded sleeve

Drawers, c1820. These were two separate leg-pieces on a draw-string. They had been customary from c1800. Previously women had worn nothing under their petticoats.

HAIRSTYLE OF 1831. Hair was dressed into most unusual shapes at this time. False side-pieces and topknots were fixed on with pins and combs.

FILIGREE BROOCH, set with topaz, early 19th century.

gloves, essential for evening wear

shorter hemline

flat satin pumps

EVENING DRESS, 1830. The style is delicately pretty. Ballet dancers' traditional long tutus originated at this time.

1817 Summer walking dress. Dresses still had high waists and narrow skirts.

1823 The waistline is returning to a more natural position.

1828 A frock coat (with a 'skirt') was now correct daywear. Padded sleeves were worn by men and women.

1829 Wider sleeves and skirts give emphasis to smaller waists. Hats are emphatic.

1829 Ankle-length single-breasted greatcoat has 'leg-of-mutton' sleeves, very full at the shoulder and tight at the wrist.

1829 The tail coat, outdoor wear in the 18th century, is now formal evening dress.

1830 Sleeves are like balloons.

1833 Winter fashion: a velvet redingote with decorated facings, worn with a bonnet with veil and a muff.

1834 Gentleman's morning dress.

1836 Sleeve fullness has slipped down the arm and is droopy, giving a more demure look. Hair is worn in a bun.

1837 Big sleeves are out, but bonnets which hide the face and flounced skirts are in for a long run of popularity.

1840 Mother and daughter. The mother's dress has the new V-shaped waistline.

1845 Out of doors, women wrapped themselves in huge shawls.

1847 Couple in winter dress.

1850   1850   1854   1856

THE CRINOLINE: 1850 TO 1870

A 'Grecian' hairpiece, 1867. False hair was very fashionable.

By the 1850s a woman needed up to five stiff petticoats to create the wide-skirted look that was admired. Their weight was a nuisance and they made the wearer hot. It was a huge relief when, in 1856, a Frenchman patented the crinoline frame, an arrangement of flexible steel hoops that held the skirt well clear of the legs. It was an immediate success. It was light and airy, and worn with only one or two petticoats beneath the dress.

The crinoline frame was worn by women of all classes, but only the rich could afford the most extravagantly decorated dresses. The middle class was now large enough to create a huge demand for fine dresses. Poorly paid women worked long hours to make them. The invention of an efficient sewing machine in 1851 made even more complicated patterns and lavish trimmings possible.

Men's clothes, in contrast, were sober. It was thought incorrect for a gentleman to wear anything conspicuous (a notion that lasted for a hundred years). Fashion's old task of impressing people with the wearer's power and glory had changed. It was now wives who wore all the finery. The vast amounts of fabric and trimmings that went into their clothes were visible proof of their husbands' riches. Men dressed for the serious business of life – trade and professional work.

Dressing in 1854. First the chemise and drawers.

Next the corset, over which goes the corset cover.

The first petticoat is a stiff fabric woven from horsehair.

small shoulder cape

evening 'uniform': black with a white shirt and tie

high neck, for daywear

centre-parted hair, and ringlets

deep 'bertha' collar

overskirt

1859

1862

1863

1867

1869

The next petticoat has rows of stitching to give a stiff effect.

Over these go one or more starched cotton petticoats.

The top petticoat is silk or lace-trimmed embroidered muslin.

Finally the dress itself adds a further layer of flounces.

EVENING and bridal wear, 1860, by Charles Worth, an Englishman who was the most fashionable dressmaker in Paris. Previously dressmakers (who might be men or women) had created clothes to order for individual clients. Worth began the system known as 'haute couture' by which a designer reproduces a limited number of copies of a dress. Such designers are called 'couturiers'.

EVENING DRESS, 1869. The skirt is narrower, with a long train behind. Overskirts were popular. This dress has a short one draped apron-wise at the front and a much longer one bunched up at the back.

AMERICAN FEMINIST Amelia Bloomer in 1850, wearing the 'bloomers' which she tried unsuccessfully to promote in place of huge skirts.

Dressing in 1860. Basic underwear, then the crinoline.

An ornamented silk petticoat covers the frame.

A dress with a ruched overskirt sits lightly on top.

drawers c1860

1850 Daytime jackets. On the left an informal style worn with casual checked trousers. Both men wear black cravats and one wears a new style of collar, turned down instead of standing up.

1850 Both sleeves and skirt of this day dress are made in tiers of flounces. Flounces could also be created by layers of skirts of varying lengths.

1854 Flounced ball gown. Its width is still achieved with petticoats.

1856 English family in outdoor clothes. The mother wears a tight-waisted jacket. Since the width of skirts made coats impractical, all manner of jackets and capes were worn. The boy is wearing a kilt, reflecting the fashion for tartan caused by Queen Victoria's enthusiasm for her Scottish home, Balmoral.

1859 The crinoline frame forms a tea-cosy-like dome around the wearer.

1862 Two men out strolling in frock coats. These were always dark, though trousers could be light coloured.

1863 The waist is higher, so that the woman's silhouette is triangular. The crinoline is now flatter in front (enabling its wearer to reach objects in front of her). The gentleman wears a suit (jacket and trousers in the same cloth) – a very casual style.

1867 Parisian town dress. Its wearer would have a carriage and had no need to worry about keeping her skirt train clean.

1869 Promenade dress, worn with some back padding, but no crinoline frame.

1871   1875   1877   1880   1880

THE BUSTLE: 1870 TO 1900

Bustle in the form of a wire cage, advertised as 'less heating to the spine than any other'.

The crinoline

frame and its huge skirts went out of fashion at the end of the 1860s. It was followed by the bustle, a small support of either horsehair fabric or a wire frame which held the skirt out at the back of a dress. This was the fashionable style until the mid 1870s. After a few years when a narrow silhouette was popular, a more exaggerated fullness at the back of the dress became the fashion in the 1880s. This look needed more support than the bustle gave and the crinolette (like a half crinoline) was invented. Separate skirts worn with blouses and jackets (the forerunner of the modern woman's suit) became popular in the 1890s. The blouses had high collars which were frequently stiffened and the jackets had wide ballooning sleeves.

Many people said that such fashions were inconvenient and that tight corsets did harm. In the late 1870s and 1880s dress reformers tried to launch simpler styles, but most women ignored them. The intricacies of fashion gave interest to their restricted lives. For some women, shopping and visits to the dressmaker were full-time activities. Pleasant hours could be spent in the luxurious department stores that were now opening, where, for the first time, all manner of fashion items could be found under one roof.

Fashions of 1878. The girl has gloves and a fashionable hat, just like her mother. The man's top hat and frock coat have altered little since the 1850s.

forward tilted hat

coils of hair at nape of neck

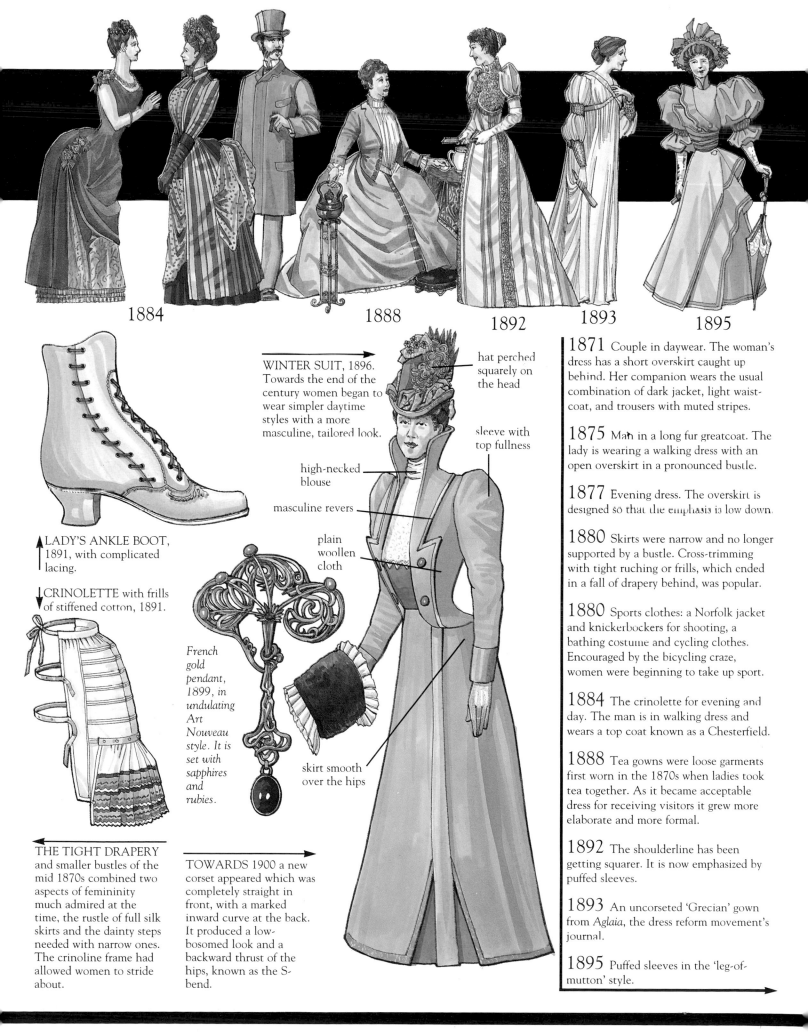

1884　　　　　1888　　1892　1893　　1895

LADY'S ANKLE BOOT, 1891, with complicated lacing.

CRINOLETTE with frills of stiffened cotton, 1891.

WINTER SUIT, 1896. Towards the end of the century women began to wear simpler daytime styles with a more masculine, tailored look.

hat perched squarely on the head

sleeve with top fullness

high-necked blouse

masculine revers

plain woollen cloth

skirt smooth over the hips

French gold pendant, 1899, in undulating Art Nouveau style. It is set with sapphires and rubies.

THE TIGHT DRAPERY and smaller bustles of the mid 1870s combined two aspects of femininity much admired at the time, the rustle of full silk skirts and the dainty steps needed with narrow ones. The crinoline frame had allowed women to stride about.

TOWARDS 1900 a new corset appeared which was completely straight in front, with a marked inward curve at the back. It produced a low-bosomed look and a backward thrust of the hips, known as the S-bend.

1871 Couple in daywear. The woman's dress has a short overskirt caught up behind. Her companion wears the usual combination of dark jacket, light waistcoat, and trousers with muted stripes.

1875 Man in a long fur greatcoat. The lady is wearing a walking dress with an open overskirt in a pronounced bustle.

1877 Evening dress. The overskirt is designed so that the emphasis is low down.

1880 Skirts were narrow and no longer supported by a bustle. Cross-trimming with tight ruching or frills, which ended in a fall of drapery behind, was popular.

1880 Sports clothes: a Norfolk jacket and knickerbockers for shooting, a bathing costume and cycling clothes. Encouraged by the bicycling craze, women were beginning to take up sport.

1884 The crinolette for evening and day. The man is in walking dress and wears a top coat known as a Chesterfield.

1888 Tea gowns were loose garments first worn in the 1870s when ladies took tea together. As it became acceptable dress for receiving visitors it grew more elaborate and more formal.

1892 The shoulderline has been getting squarer. It is now emphasized by puffed sleeves.

1893 An uncorseted 'Grecian' gown from *Aglaia*, the dress reform movement's journal.

1895 Puffed sleeves in the 'leg-of-mutton' style.

1901   1905   1908   1909   1910   1912

THE LAST OF LUXURY

— boater

The new-style shorter corset of 1908, designed to give a slim but natural figure.

The period before World War One was the last in which fashion was primarily for wealthy people with leisure to fill their time with such activities as a social season spent in London, weekend house-parties in the country and winter visits to foreign resorts. Each activity needed different clothes, and the rules were strict about what was worn at various times. Rich people changed their clothes up to six times a day. A valet or lady's maid got everything ready for them.

Most men still wore frock coats and top hats in town, though lounge suits and homburg hats were permitted. Tweeds and sports clothes were for the country. Black tail coats were for formal dinners, dinner jackets for dining at home.

After 1900 women's fashions demanded full-bosomed figures. Skirts, which flared out at the hem, were made of soft fabrics trimmed with lots of lace. The S-bend figure then became straighter, and in 1908 the French couturier Paul Poiret introduced almost waistless dresses. He said he was freeing women from the corset! His skirts next grew very narrow. The Russian Ballet, a sensation in Paris in 1910, inspired his gaudy 'oriental' dresses, topped with turbans and plumes.

Then came the war. Afterwards fashions were created for a quite different kind of life.

THREE 1910 VERSIONS of the tailored suit, with long jackets and narrow 'hobble' skirts. Each woman wears an emphatic hat and carries a fur muff or stole. Tailored suits first became popular at the end of the 19th century and were worn by the more independent woman. Active women often eased these skirts with concealed pleating. The man, in morning coat and pin-striped trousers, is dressed for a formal daytime occasion.

Hats, loaded with flowers or feathers, became bigger as skirts narrowed.

1913 **1914** **1915** **1916** **1918** **1919** **1919**

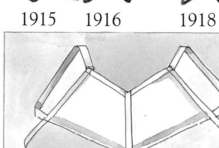

1910 hobble garters used by women who wore hobble skirts, to stop themselves taking long steps and splitting the seams.

A new undergarment, the brassière, 1914. The bust needed separate support because corsets no longer came high enough up the body to do the job.

English diamond pendant

OSTRICH FEATHERS were a popular trimming for collars, cuffs, fans and hats, and were curled and made into long feather scarves, known as boas.

FASHIONABLE HATS, 1916. Hats were smaller, eccentrically shaped, and often brimless. They were usually worn at rakish angles.

1901 Dressed for the country. Her large hat, 'choker' collar, and low sloping bosom (shaped by her corset), are just as turn-of-the-century fashion demanded. A country visit meant a gentle promenade in your host and hostess's grounds, not the long energetic walks accepted today.

1905 Fashionable motoring clothes.

1908 Paul Poiret converted the fashionable shape from a tight-waisted hour-glass into a swathed tube.

1909 For the less well off, paper patterns were available by post. This summer style from Butterick is a watered-down version of the new narrow look.

1910 Long ermine cape and matching muff, edged with skunk fur.

1912 Bridesmaid's dress, with a new plunging V neckline.

1913 Wrap-over skirts made walking in narrow styles less difficult.

1914 Overtunics were fashionable on dresses and suits.

1915 Wartime tram conductress.

1916 Factory worker in overalls. Trousers for women would have been a sensation, but in wartime they were accepted as a common-sense measure.

1918 Raincoat with raglan sleeves.

1919 Ready to wear English suit.

1919 Evening dress. During the war skirts had risen to mid calf.

1921　　　1922　　　1923　　1924　　　1925

THE TWENTIES

Vanity case, 1925, for mirror, powder and lipstick. Women now retouched their faces in public.

Corselette, 1926. Elasticated fabric, which appeared in the 1930s, made these garments much more comfortable.

bobbed hair, with deep 'Marcel' wave

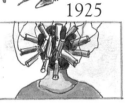

Having a 'permanent wave', 1921. The hair was crimped by an electric machine, a long, hot process. Below, the result.

Women led

active lives and did responsible jobs during World War One. Afterwards, the idea that a fashionable woman had little to think about apart from clothes seemed hopelessly outdated. Younger women especially wanted more independence – to work before they married, perhaps even to live on their own if they could afford it. Twenties designers responded with styles that suggested youth and freedom. Corsets were tossed away. The new shape was completely flat and garments resembled loose tubes. In the early Twenties dresses were long, but in the hands of French couturiers like Lanvin, Doucet and Vionnet, these simple shapes had great charm. Hemlines then rose and were at their shortest around 1926, though never above the knee. Short skirts and the new bold use of bright cosmetics shocked the older generation.

There were other reasons for welcoming simpler styles. Since the war it had become harder to find servants to look after delicate clothes. Working-class women did not want to be servants when they could work in factories and offices. Ordinary people began to dress more fashionably, thanks to cheap ready-to-wear clothes. Manufacturers realized big profits could be made supplying these new customers with smart styles.

corselette

Short skirts gave legs greater importance. Stockings were flesh-coloured and transparent. Silk ones were the most luxurious, otherwise they were 'lisle' (artificial silk).

suspenders

silk stockings

CLOCHE HAT, 1925. These appeared in 1923 and for the next five years were the only smart headwear. They were pulled down over the eyebrows.

EVENING WEAR, 1926. Evening dresses were as short as day clothes, and often had plunging necklines at the back, and sometimes at the front as well. Though the overall look was boyish, the details were feminine, like these ruffles, scallops and little frills.

1925 **1926** **1927** **1928** **1928** **1928** **1929** **1929**

Women had their hair cut short (bobbed) to give a neat neckline with cloche hats. Then came the boyish 'shingle', worn by the woman on the right.

Men's daywear was becoming less formal, but evening dress was little changed.

shingled hair

lipstick

silk stockings

asymmetric hemline

1921 Coat dress and fox fur stole.

1922 Two men in elegant daywear raise their hats (top hats are no longer required by day) to a mother and child wearing styles by the French couturier Jeanne Lanvin. The child's hat style is about to become adult fashion.

1923 A coat trimmed with fur in the slender line of the moment.

1924 Casual checked jacket over a calf-length dress with side pleats.

1925 Evening dress in silk chiffon heavily embroidered with glass beads.

1925 Evening dress by Coco Chanel, the couturier who made extremely simple clothes highly fashionable.

1926 Women's skirts had never been so short. The overall boyish look is emphasized by close-cropped hair.

1927 In Britain, Edward Prince of Wales popularized sweaters, plus-fours and brogues.

1928 Fur-trimmed evening coat. Hemlines are becoming longer again.

1928 Clinging, bias-cut evening dress by Madeleine Vionnet.

1928 Short skirts (like this filmy day dress) or long? People were in two minds.

1929 Afternoon dress and jacket of velvet trimmed with monkey fur.

1929 A compromise: an evening dress with a short hem and a long train.

1930　　　1930　　　1930　　　1931　　　　1932　　　1933　　　　1933

The Thirties

Lip-shaped button, a typically witty touch from designer, Elsa Schiaparelli.

B y 1930 the boyish look had given way to softer, more fluid styles. The waist had returned but was not emphasized; skirts were calf length and often bias cut, slim on the hips and gently flaring at the hem. From the mid Thirties daytime styles became sharper, with pleats and wide padded shoulders, and in 1939 short skirts reappeared.

Fashion became less exclusive. Through the popularity of magazines and the emergence of the ready-made clothing industry more women were able to see and buy stylish clothes. Cinema, too, was an important influence. Many women tried to look like a favourite film star.

Fashion drawings show that the ideal Thirties' figure was tall and slender, but photographs of models in beachwear prove that what seemed slim then would appear quite hefty now. The women look robust and energetic, reflecting the new enthusiasm for outdoor life. Sunbathing was the latest health craze, and beachwear was designed to expose much more flesh. More people were playing sports or going into the countryside for weekend hikes. They wore practical skirts and jerseys, shirts and shorts. Fashion took up the theme, and a new type of casual clothing appeared for men and women, not intended for any particular sport but free and easy to wear.

1931 LEISUREWEAR: sleeveless top and wide-legged 'slacks' as seen at smart resorts on the French Riviera. Women only wore trousers for sport, beach or trendy parties.

peroxide blonde

COUPLE DANCING, 1931. Low backed or even backless dresses were a favourite form of evening wear. Bias-cut satin was used for a sleek, smooth line, that followed the curves of the body.

1934

1935

1936

1938

1938

1939

1935 brooch or clips

Paris dresses in 1937. The skirts are quite long and smooth over the hips, but the shoulders are square, and the decoration angular and fussy. A well-dressed woman wears a hat in town. Hats are small and often worn tilted, with the brim pulled over one eye.

1938 brooch or clips

Two clips which could be linked as a brooch and worn at the neck of a dress were popular.

box-pleated hem

fox fur stole

court shoes

elaborate neckline detail

1930 A ready-made lace dress and matching 'coatee' produced a lady-like effect that was very popular.

1930 Knitwear cardigan suit. Casual styles catered for more outdoor women.

1930 Formal wear remained important. A 'little black dress' was essential.

1931 The woman is in beach pyjamas, but women were also sunbathing in costumes similar to the man's.

1932 For casual summer wear a dress was no longer necessary.

1933 Clothes for smart holidays abroad.

1933 Evening dress. In place of the customary tail coat and white bow tie, men can now wear a black tie and dinner jacket at all but the most formal events.

1934 Town wear: formal dark overcoat and bowler hat; long afternoon dress in a floral print and, of course, gloves.

1935 Backless evening dress. Inset gores of material give the hip-hugging skirt a rippling train.

1936 Travelling clothes. The man wears a waterproof overcoat; the woman's coat is cut on masculine lines.

1938 A fox-fur collar emphasizes this coat's broad-shouldered look.

1938 Fashionably covered-up evening dress with padded shoulders.

1939 Fashion for the last year of peace.

1941   1942   1942   1943   1943   1944   1946

THE FORTIES

French hat made of wood-shavings, 1941. During the war designers made use of whatever materials they could lay hands on.

From 1940 to 1945 World War Two absorbed all resources. Raw materials became scarce because overseas trade was at a standstill: factories made only armaments, uniforms and supplies. All the nations involved suffered shortages, and Europe endured extreme hardship. It was no time for fashion. Cloth was in short supply, and the British government rationed clothes by giving people a limited number of coupons to buy them with. It also introduced 'Utility' regulations stating what styles were allowed, how much cloth could go into a garment, and what it must cost. There was even a button quota; you could not have them at the wrists.

Women made the best of things. They wore vivid lipstick, made headscarves into turbans, re-knitted woollies, and painted fake stockings on bare legs. In America things were easier, and stockings made of nylon, a wonderful new artificial fibre, were a treat brought by American forces to fashion-starved Europe.

Americans had their home-grown fashion during the war years, but afterwards the French made a determined effort to regain the fashion lead. In 1947 the couturier Christian Dior introducd a style so startlingly different from what women were used to that it was immediately dubbed 'The New Look'. It was an instant success.

MOST MEN now wore separate vest and pants instead of old-fashioned combinations. But women had taken to all-in-one camiknickers.

hat in man's 'trilby' style

shoulder bag

silk camiknickers

WARTIME 'UTILITY' suit. Styles were square-shouldered with narrow or skimpily pleated skirts just covering the knees. Many women now wore trousers (known as slacks) to save on stockings.

nylon stockings

1946   1946   1946   1947   1948   1948   1949

'waspie' girdle

DIOR'S 'NEW LOOK',
1947. After the dreary war
years, its swirling skirts
and feminine outline were
irresistible. Shoulders
were rounded and waists
tiny.

neat off-the-
face hat

'THE NEW LOOK'
meant women needed
new underwear – a full
waist petticoat, and a tight-
waisted 'waspie' girdle – to
give the right shape.

MAN'S LOUNGE SUIT,
1948. The postwar look
for men was wide in the
shoulders and legs. A
double- or single-breasted
lounge suit, with bowler
hat or trilby, could be
worn on most occasions.

round-toed
court shoes

SOME KILL-JOYS
criticized the 'New Look'
for its extravagant use of
material, which was still
in short supply in many
countries.

1941 Utility dress in 'Viyella', a blend
of wool and cotton.

1942 A wartime bride wears a smart
boxy suit.

1942 Jacket and slacks, from a 'Utility'
fashion show. Women in trousers were
now an everyday sight.

1943 A design condemned by the
British Board of Trade for using
unnecessary buttons. It was not produced.

1943 Fashions from occupied France.

1944 American serviceman. For many
men uniform was the only option.

1946 The postwar wide-shouldered,
short-skirted look.

1946 A 'tailor made', a woman's suit
hand-tailored like a man's.

1946 Film star Rita Hayworth dressed
by American couturier Adrian.

1946 French model, in a Lanvin coat,
has Hayworth-style long hair and peep-
toed shoes with platform soles.

1947 Dior's 'New Look'.

1948 Dior suit with trend-setting
three-quarter sleeves, fly-away cuffs and
long narrow skirt.

1948 Clothes for a grand occasion.
The man wears tails, the woman a satin
evening dress by Charles James, a British-
born designer working in New York.

1949 French dress with 'pencil' skirt.

1950   1952   1953   1953   1953   1954   1955

THE FIFTIES

Stiletto-heeled shoes: an Italian idea. Italy became a fashion force in the Fifties.

As the world

became normal again in the 1950s there seemed no reason why fashion should not go on as in the past, with clothes for lunch parties, cocktails, dinner, the theatre and with unwritten rules about what was worn when. Couturiers launched styles which gave manufacturers ideas to copy. Dior based some of his fashion shapes on letters, producing the 'H line' (straight up and down), the 'A line' (wide at the bottom) and the 'Y line (wide at the top). Skirts were pencil slim or full. By the late Fifties they were shorter, with full ones worn over nylon petticoats as stiff as lampshades.

Couturiers' clothes were designed to suit women well over twenty years old. Fashion had always been for adults, as only they could afford it. Youngsters, being low earners or dependent on their parents, were ignored by designers. But in the booming Fifties young people earned good wages while still living at home. Often they had more spare cash than their parents. The Americans coined a name for them: 'teenagers'. They liked jive, rock and roll and casual clothes, and they did not want to look like their elders. The American fashion industry recognized this huge new market and started making styles especially for them. Young fashion, born in America, was about to change the fashion world.

THE LADY-LIKE LOOK: cotton summer dress, 1951. The lingering influence of the New Look kept tight-waisted, full-skirted dresses in favour throughout the Fifties, usually in clear 'pretty' colours and bold patterns. Dresses were soon appearing in new man-made fibres, such as polyester and acrylic.

hair in neat curls

cap sleeves

cotton gloves, even on hot days

small waist

Strapless bra, wired to hold its shape. Large busts were admired in the Fifties.

dirndl skirt

1956   1957   1958   1958   1959   1959

Teenage fashion, 1952: tapering trousers, jersey-knit cotton top and moccasins. Chunky sweaters were also worn.

Casual fashions often develop from work clothes. Jeans were originally tough trousers for 19th-century gold-miners.

polo neck

FILM STAR James Dean was the role model for a generation of teenagers. No film clothes have been as influential as his denim jeans in 1955.

three-quarter sleeves

SETTING HAIR on rollers, the plastic tubes that produced the bounced-out hair-styles of the late Fifties. The 'beehive' was a favourite: the hair was pulled up, backcombed and pinned to form a tall mound.

Y-fronts were introduced in the Fifties.

ankle zips

1950 Strapless evening dress. Its bodice was boned to hold it up. Flat-chested women had to take care that the swing of the big skirt did not pull the bodice round, so that its padded bust ended up under the armpit.

1952 Teenage calf-length 'pedal-pushers' became a fashion for all.

1953 British 'Teddy boy' in velvet-collared coat, string tie and sideburns.

1953 Teenage fashion. Circular skirts were ideal for jiving.

1953 Suits moulded to the figure needed a flat stomach and firm buttocks. Even young women wore stiffened elasticated 'roll-ons' to achieve this.

1954 Cotton summer dress.

1955 Dior's A-line silhouette.

1956 Evening clothes. Cummerbunds enlivened men's dinner jackets.

1957 The woman wears a startling new style from France: the sack dress. It was cut to blouse out at the back and narrow to the hem.

1958 The 'trapeze' look: shorter than the A-line, it hung from the shoulders.

1958 The fashionable bloused-backed outline of the trapeze look.

1959 Short overcoats for men, and for women shorter skirts.

1959 Cocktail dress by French couturier Yves Saint Laurent.

39

1961   1962   1965   1966   1966   1967   1969   1969

THE SIXTIES AND SEVENTIES

Miniskirts required the briefest of underwear. Cotton briefs and tights were the order of the day.

In the Sixties

the focus of fashion changed. No longer were designers aiming at the sophisticated older woman, but at her daughters. If you look at Fifties' fashion magazines you will notice how matronly the models seem (though they may have been quite young). The reason for the change was simple. The thousands of young working women had money to spend and wanted their own styles. The fashion industry was quick to sense this and produced young styles for them. It was glamorous to look spindly and adolescent. Youthful mini-skirts became the only smart thing to wear, and by 1966 hems had risen to mid thigh. This had a great effect on fashion and everybody, even older women, wore skirts which showed their knees.

In 1969 the ankle-length maxi-coat appeared. It was a short-lived style, but it made long skirts – or any length of skirt – an option that is still around. In the Sixties and Seventies the Paris couturiers ceased to set the fashions. Instead, bright young designers of many nationalities exploited anything in the news – hippies, 'outer space', punks – to produce a bewildering variety of styles. There were 'fun' and 'ethnic' clothes: caftans and Turkish trousers, see-through tops and hot pants. In the Seventies you could 'do your own thing', and wear almost anything anywhere.

MINIDRESSES by French designer, Yves Saint Laurent 1965. Their geometrical patterns are inspired by modern art.

heavy eye make-up

tight-fitting underarms

40

1970   1971   1972   1975   1977   1979

WOMEN DID their best to look like top British model Twiggy, who was seventeen and as thin as a stick. Dieting became a beauty fad.

THE 1968 'ROMANTIC' look for men. In the new fashion climate men were free to take an interest in clothes again.

platform-sole shoe

hair bounced out by rollers

TROUSER SUIT, 1972. It was the answer to many dress problems, until its popularity with older women made it seem dowdy.

Seventies punks. From the mid Seventies this way of dressing was part of the lifestyle of some teenagers. There were other groups with their own styles, but the punks made the headlines in what became known as 'street fashion'. Top designers took some of their ideas to use for smart expensive clothes.

1961 The style made famous by Jacqueline Kennedy: a neat outline, slightly shaped to the chest, with three-quarter sleeves closely fitting at the armpits.

1962 Bold Italian 'pant suit': tunic, drainpipe trousers, pumps, each differently patterned.

1965 'Mod' gear from Carnaby Street, London: peaked cap, hipster pants, and turtle neck in place of a tie.

1966 Mary Quant's miniskirt with daisy-patterned tights.

1966 Velvet trouser suit for evening wear. Trouser suits came in all kinds of fabric. Uncrushable 'Crimplene' versions became a stand-by of the not so smart.

1967 The miniskirt at its height.

1969 A variety of hemlines, in the year of the maxi-coat.

1969 Hippy clothes, part of the Californian free and easy lifestyle of the late Sixties, were copied by high fashion.

1970 Long swirling skirts were a reaction to the mini.

1971 Young people wore jeans almost non-stop. The Seventies shape was flares.

1972 Hot-pants. For a couple of years these were even acceptable at the office.

1975 Man with 'kipper' tie; woman in romantic cotton dress by Laura Ashley.

1977 Expensive punk-inspired dress, with exquisitely stitched tatters.

1979 Evening dress by influential Japanese designer Kenzo.

1982   1983   1983   1984   1986   1987

THE EIGHTIES AND NINETIES

In the Eighties status-symbol accessories, like this Gucci handbag, were all-important.

DESIGNER WEAR, 1982. Men's expensive Italian casuals in suede.

EXERCISE GEAR, 1982. The sweatshirt has detachable shoulder pads, so it is really a fashion garment.

stud neck-fastening

zippered pocket

loose sweatshirt

leggings

trainers

In the Eighties

and Nineties fashion writers have written about 'looks' rather than about styles or shapes as they used to when couturiers decided fashion: the sporty look, the granny look – even 'grunge', the poor look. 'Power dressing' was a look of the Eighties boom. Wide-shouldered suits suggesting authority were worn by men and women who wanted to seem successful. People became fitness fanatics, and Lycra cycling shorts became smart casual wear.

The Nineties are still here, and it is harder to pick out present trends than past ones. Today's fashions do not have to be luxurious, like those of princes long ago, or extravagant and impractical, like those rich women once wore. They do not suggest high social class, or even money (unless they have a smart designer label). Then why do people bother with fashion? Because to have the newest look shows that they are 'in the know'. To be out of fashion is not to keep up with the times. In our competitive world keeping up or, even better, keeping ahead, matters to most people. This is why we scan the fashion pages and riffle through the stock in the shops: we want to make sure we recognize that 'look'. One thing is certain: it will not seem the right look for long.

1990 1990 1991 1992 1992 1993 1994 1994

PUTTING CLOTHES together for the 1990s look. His: trousers with battledress pockets, traditional jacket and waistcoat, a cardigan instead of a shirt. Hers: ribbed vest, Indian-collared shirt, long denim jacket, sarong-tied trousers.

NINETIES VERSION of the formal tailored suit: single-breasted fitted jacket and swinging mini kilt by Italian designer Gianni Versace.

7-denier nylon tights

1982 Athletes' tracksuits became fashionable through the jogging craze.

1983 Clothes that fell off the shoulders, designed by Jean-Paul Gaultier.

1983 Men's styles for women by American designer Calvin Klein.

1984 Casual winter wear made of waterproofed cotton for the whole family.

1986 Clothes by Italian designer Giorgio Armani, the designer name most favoured by younger power-dressers.

1987 Shell suits were smart exercise garments that plunged downmarket to appear in garish prints or pastel-shades.

1990 Mail order fashion clothes. Some catalogues offer value and real style.

1990 Fashionable skirts were above the knee or well below the calf.

1991 Striped tank top and matching cycling shorts in cotton and Lycra.

1992 Baggy coat and draw-string shorts. Styles clung, or hung very loose.

1992 Designer-label Italian work-out gear, simple but astronomically expensive.

1993 Linen dress by Japanese designer, Rei Kawakubo of Comme des Garçons.

1994 Designer outfit in linen. A suit without a tie can now be smart (if it is a fashionable suit).

1994 Sheath dress that takes its style from sportswear.

FASHION FACTS

According to the Bible, leatherwear was the world's first fashion. Genesis chapter 3 records that God provided Adam and Eve with coats of skins before sending them out of the Garden of Eden. This is a reasonable description of the sort of clothes our earliest ancestors wore, though until they had thought of making needles of bone and thread from animal sinews, the coats could only have been wrap-around.

An Assyrian law of c1200 BC compelled women to wear veils whenever they went out. This is the first known mention of a custom still followed in parts of the Middle East.

In ancient Greece only the upper classes were supposed to wear bright colours. In the 5th century BC the Greek historian Herodotus mentions that an Athenian decree forbad working people to appear in public in dyed clothes.

Some Romans of the 1st century BC still believed in the old-fashioned simplicity and plain homespun clothing of earlier times. Julius Caesar (101-44 BC) aroused adverse comment by wearing a tunic with a patterned hem and sleeve-bands.

The early Christian bishops were shocked by the what they considered to be the gaudy finery of late Roman fashion. In the 3rd century AD one of them declared 'God would have made purple sheep if he had wished woollen clothes to be purple'.

Medieval poetry was a source of fashion guidance. The *Roman de la Rose* (1225) advised women to wear false hair shaped into rolls and horns, and to leave their gowns open 'a good half foot' at the front and back.

The horned head-dresses that women wore in the late Middle Ages outraged Church leaders. They condemned the shape as devilish, and 'stuffed with the hair of dead women who may be in hell'. The Bishop of Paris encouraged people to shout insults at women wearing them.

When starching came in, in the 1560s, it literally went to people's heads, in the form of increasingly wide ruffs. In 1578 Henri III of France appeared in such a huge starched ruff that the people of Paris said he looked like John the Baptist with his head on a plate.

The first time it was possible to see pictures of the latest fashions was in 1770, when the English periodical *The Lady's Magazine* began to publish fashion plates. Before then people had to wait for fashion news to trickle through. Dressmakers used to tour the country visiting clients to show them dolls dressed in the newest styles. European fashion dolls were sent to the American colonies.

In the early 19th century Beau Brummell (1778-1840), the British dandy and close friend of the Prince Regent, was the unchallenged authority on matters of male elegance. He was so exacting that he had the thumbs of his gloves cut by one firm and the fingers by another, to ensure a perfect fit.

The hugely successful 19th-century couturier, Charles Worth, was extremely high-handed with customers, and turned them away if they did not come with a good recommendation. The great ladies of Parisian society begged him to design for them, however rude he was.

Just think of the problem of washing corsets! We know that 19th-century corsets went rusty in the wash because rust-proof ones were advertised.

The Irish playwright, Oscar Wilde (1856-1900), defined fashion, which at that time meant the restrictive styles of the 1880s, as a 'a form of ugliness so intolerable that we have to alter it every six months'.

Denim jeans are known as Levis because they were invented by Levi Strauss, a Bavarian-born American immigrant who went to try his luck in the 1850s Californian goldrush. He didn't find gold, but he did make a fortune supplying the miners with hard-wearing work trousers. His first pairs were made from tent canvas but later he used denim, a tough French cloth from Nîmes ('de Nîmes' in French), which he dyed blue. In 1873 he patented the idea of reinforcing pockets and seams with copper rivets.

Zip fasteners were developed from an idea patented in Chicago, USA, in 1893. The first zips that really worked appeared in 1913 on money belts and tobacco pouches. They did not make fashion headlines until the early Thirties when Schiaparelli, the Italian-born designer who loved quirky details, used big zips as decoration on garments.

GLOSSARY

Bias cut Way of cutting fabric across its weave, so it moulds to the body or flares out.

Bicorne hat Hat with its brim turned up on both sides and folded flat against the crown.

Bowler hat Hard hat with a round crown and a brim curved up at the sides.

Burgundian Belonging to Burgundy, an area of east central France. In the Middle Ages it was an independent state ruled by a duke, controlling most of modern Holland, Belgium and Luxembourg.

Carnaby Street in London's West End, famous in the 1960s for selling young fashions.

Chemise A man's undershirt, or a woman's long undergarment.

Chiffon Light gauzy fabric, usually silk.

Cocked hat Hat with the brim turned up in three places, giving it a triangular shape.

Codpiece Flap or bag of material in the front of men's hose that filled the gap at the top between the two leg pieces.

Combinations Men's long-legged, all-in-one undergarment.

Court shoe Women's plain, high-heeled, low-fronted shoe.

Crimplene Crinkly, uncrushable fabric of man-made fibre, developed by ICI in the 1960s.

Cummerbund Wide pleated waist sash.

Denier Measurement of the fineness of yarn. Used since the 19th century for silk, it is now also used for synthetic fibres, tights and stockings.

Dirndl skirt A gathered skirt which can be cut on the cross or straight of the fabric.

Ermine The silky white winter fur of the stoat.

Fillet Strip of material tied around the head.

Flemish Belonging to the area known in the Middle Ages as Flanders, an independent state occupying parts of modern France and Belgium.

Franks A Germanic people who gained control of a large area of what is now France and Germany when the Roman empire collapsed in the 5th century.

Girdle Lightweight, boneless elastic corset with suspenders, introduced in the 1920s.

Gores Triangular pieces of material inserted in a garment to give extra fullness in certain places.

Homburg hat Hat with a narrow brim, a deep crease in the crown and a wide hatband.

Horsehair Stiff fabric woven from horses' mane and tail hair.

Jerkin A garment similar to a doublet, and sometimes worn over it.

Kipper tie A very broad tie, worn in the 1970s.

Lounge suit Daytime suit of matching jacket, trousers and waistcoat. It appeared in the 1870s as a casual style and is now a formal one.

Lycra A stretch fabric introduced in 1958 by the American firm Du Pont, and originally used for underwear.

Mary Quant English designer associated with the miniskirt and other young fashions in the 1960s.

Marcel wave Hairstyle with deep waves made by special curling tongs and lasting a few days. It was invented in 1872 by French hairdresser Marcel.

Merovingian The time of the first Frankish kings who ruled what is today France and parts of Germany, from the 5th to the 8th centuries.

Mods British teenagers of the late 1950s and early 1960s who favoured a neat appearance.

Page-boy hairstyle A woman's hairstyle, with shoulder-length hair turned under at the ends.

Pantaloons Very tight-fitting trousers, popular from 1800 to 1850.

Pattens Wooden under-shoes.

Peroxide blonde Someone with artificially blonde hair, achieved by bleaching it with peroxide of hydrogen.

Plus-fours 1920s term for very baggy knee breeches worn by men on sporting occasions.

Pumps Light, flat-heeled shoes.

Roll-on Elasticated girdle without suspenders.

Shift Originally an undergarment; also used to describe a plain straight dress.

Sideburns Facial hair which men allow to grow down the sides of their cheeks.

Stole A long wide scarf, worn round the body.

Surcoat Medieval overtunic, sometimes sleeveless.

Teddy boy A member of the first group of young people to invent a 'street fashion', in Britain in the late 1940s and 1950s. They wore their own version of turn-of-the-century 'Edwardian' styles.

Whalebone A horny substance from the upper jaw of the whale.

Wimple A piece of fine white cloth which women wore below the chin and covering the neck, in the 13th and 14th centuries.

Winklepickers Men's very sharply pointed shoes.

INDEX